Odes to Loc

...and other musings

By
Paola Bradley

MAPLE
PUBLISHERS

Odes to Lockdown

Author: Paola Bradley

Copyright © Paola Bradley (2022)

The right of Paola Bradley to be identified as author of this work has been asserted by the author in accordance with section 77 and 78 of the Copyright, Designs and Patents Act 1988.

First Published in 2022

ISBN 978-1-915492-96-8 (Paperback)
      978-1-915492-97-5 (E-Book)

Book Cover Design and Layout by:
    Maple Publishers
    www.maplepublishers.com

Published by:
    Maple Publishers
    1 Brunel Way,
    Slough,
    SL1 1FQ, UK
    www.maplepublishers.com

Contents

PANDEMIC

The silence hurt
The empty hours
Aching to be filled
With meaningful activity
With encouraging words
The office abandoned
The empty desks
Unread bookcases
Files to be scrutinised
Would things ever revert?
The hubbub of colleagues
The banter in the corridor
The incidental exchange of ideas
The shared insights on the whiteboard
The feeling of team
A form of family
All a distant memory
Not a worthy competitor
Not a godforsaken war
Not a foreign power
But an infinitesimally small
Invisible enemy
Out of nowhere
Has changed everything
Causing a revolution
In the path of evolution
Economy thwarted
Jobs lost
Education abandoned
Caught us all by surprise

Made us hunker in our homes
Afraid to come out
Hiding behind screens
Hiding behind masks
Scrubbing hands religiously
Avoiding those we hold dear
Each interpreting the guidelines differently
Applying tailored logic
Trust breached
Will life ever return to where it was?

COVID Solace

The days are drawing in
Darkness befalling
Literal and metaphorical
Closing this challenging year
So far from the perfect
2020 hindsight billed
If mental health wasn't already an issue
This year has tested us all
With no clear end in sight
The bleakest of times
When all the news is negative
An infinitesimally small enemy
Lay hostage to our world
Not just COVID symptoms
But depression and anxiety increased
A battle with loneliness fought daily
But it is against this backdrop
In the most difficult of times
That superheroes are revealed
Those who step up to the plate
Regardless the prognosis is poor
Let the spotlight fall on
Our online community group
The beacon of light
Solace and company
Structure and challenge
Filling an otherwise empty week
With diverse opportunities
To engage and entertain

Friendly supportive faces
An extended family has emerged
The common threads
Our shared cultural and religious roots
Respectfully expressed in different ways
Also, our mental health scars
No need to disclose
Yet accepted and unjudged
The weekly packed programme
A valued lifeline
Making each day a little brighter
Leaving each of us better equipped
And facing tomorrow less daunting

Paola Bradley

NO PLACE LIKE...

Some people love castles
Some rolling countryside
Lakes or palm-fringed beaches
The dynamic bustle of markets
The tranquility of the forest
The drama of safari
Or appreciate the majesty of skyscrapers
Kissing the clouds in the sky
We travel far and spend great sums
To feast our eyes on nature
Or marvel at the feats of fellow man
The edifices of today and long ago
But where do I now feel most comfortable?
Most alive and in my skin?
Which space the most sacred
A temple to revel in?
My home is my haven
My laptop a portal to expansion
Visiting virtual vistas
Tasting new horizons
Exploring beyond my means
Without leaving the comfort
Of my favourite arm chair
My imagination and index finger
The only possible limitations
To experiencing and relishing the new

ABSENCE

Let's start with what I don't miss
The commute and daily grime
What I do miss in different ways
Is how to occupy and fill my time
FaceTime and Zoom
Temporarily fill my room
But absent are the hugs
The cuddles and the kisses
Probably the things
Most everybody misses
These days a week can go by
Without one friendly face to spy
I miss the conversations
The fripperies and chatter
What I earnestly long for now
Is a long inane gossip or natter
Instead I face a wall of silence
You could hear a pin drop
How can life be so quiet?
How can the noise just completely stop?
Friends have mostly retrenched
Back to their nuclear families
Real families busied and absent
With different conflicting priorities
I have had to learn to amuse myself and cope alone
Buried in my books, my laptop and my phone
I wouldn't have chosen this lonely solitary life
But on reflection it is better
Far better than still being a wife

LIVING THE DREAM

Through the seasons in your life
What matters changes
In first flush of youth
Scholarly accolades count
Belonging in your social circle
The right trainers and hoodie
Maturity shifts needs and priorities
A good job,
Nice home, new car
Two point four children
A holiday in the sun
With greying temples
New desires dawn,
Focus changes
A slower burn
Less immediate
Horizons pushed farther
Appreciating each day
Of life and love
And sound knees
Marvelling at nature
And the new generations
Living the dream
No longer about material pleasures
More simple ones magnified
By the lens of time
And the knowledge
That each today is unrepeatable
And each tomorrow is precious

SLOW NEWS CYCLE

Today there is no drama
Today there is no war
Today there is no raging virus
Today there is no scandal
The newsreader shuffle papers
They grasp vainly for potent words
No raised eyebrows
No solemn pauses
No inflection of gravitas
Instead we passively consume fripperies
Frothy human interstate's snippets
The hilarity of misshapen veg
Pets misbehaving wildly
Popstars faring worse
Politicians' rubber faces
Spewing irrelevant nonsense
Blah blah blah
The news blares from the tv
Flashing images summarily ignored
We have become immune
Self-protection from the hubris
Nothing shocks us any more
Nothing moves us
Our emotional constipation obvious
Oblivious to realities
Too wrapped up in our own lives
To notice or to care
Today may be a slow news cycle
Tomorrow may bring calamity

Paola Bradley

But we are conditioned to ignore
The words and images beamed into our homes
Insulated from actualities
The news doesn't touch us
Until eventually it does

THE TORCH

It's late
Or at least it feels that way
It's day
Or at least it seems that way
Summarily sent to bed
School looms tomorrow
Duvet crisp and fragrant
Pillows downy and plump
Sleep somehow eludes me
Slumber dimly distant
I hear my parents talking
Above the TV blaring
Now we're out of earshot
I'm sure I hear them swearing
I know I should be sleeping
Or tomorrow heavy lids
And dark circles will betray me
Ordinarily, now I would be dreaming
But tonight, I see no solution
Other than reach for my dogeared novel
And hunker furtively beneath the covers
A trusty torch to illuminate
Words sear into my imagination
Conjuring a world
To distract, enchant and delight
Brought into focus
By my little pocket light
I hope it makes me sleepy

I hope it makes me yawn
Heralding dreams galore
And the only sound to be heard from me
Is a loud, contented snore

NEIGHBOURS

We live side by side
In identical houses
Leading parallel lives
You in your home
Me in mine
I see you every day
Same place
Similar time
Different clothes
Fresh hair and make-up
We exchange pleasantries
The weather, family, health
Superficial details shared
The illusion of connectedness
Furthered and maintained
As we fill in random gaps
In the tapestry of our lives
We scurry away
Me back to my house
You back to yours
As the front door closes
I imagine your life
And wonder fleetingly
Is it easier than mine?
Are you happy?
Are you more fulfilled?
Are your whites whiter?
Then I re-immerse myself in today

Thoughts of you set aside
For now, at least
In the knowledge that tomorrow
The cycle will rinse and repeat
And our paths will cross again

ADVICE TO A YOUNGER ME

Hindsight is marvellous
Wisdom surely acquired
If I knew back then
What I know now
My life could truly
Have been inspired
Stupid choices I made
Bad decisions you see
The folly of youth
Detrimental as can be
Self-assured and stubborn
Foolish and arrogant
Carefree and indignant
There was no telling me
Impervious to advice
Repelling wise counsel
So sure of myself
And the self-lies I'd tell
My cocoon of self-confidence
Shielded me from reality
Blinded me from the truth
Obscured the obvious
Made black seem white
It really wasn't right
Now I look back
Not with charity
Not with pity

But with sadness
And a heavy heart
Living now with my consequences
Of a life blown apart

ART

Beauty is in the eye of the beholder
Wonky lines, dabs and smears
Displayed on a canvas
Interpretation a perspective
I see chaos
You see meaning
I see an ugly mess
You see art
I ponder at the abstraction
You perceive form
I struggle to understand
You marvel knowingly
Here we both stand
Two clashing perspectives
Neither right,
Neither wrong
But each convinced
Sure we are correct
Failing to comprehend
The alternative viewpoint
Clinging to our narrative
Closed to a different understanding
Same input, different output
A metaphor for life punishment

PUNISHMENT

Wearing an orange jumpsuit
Liberty cruelly taken
I ponder my life
Its direction, now misshapen
Not a deed
Not an actual act
Not a transgression
The sad and shocking fact
Given my mazel
Given my luck
I'm on death row
What the f—?!
Wrong time
Wrong place
Wrong conclusion
Wrong face
Twelve jurors
Supposedly strong and true
Made a catastrophic mistake
What's to do?
I trusted my brief
I trusted the law
But now I'm banged up
My life gone from before
Gone is my freedom
Gone is my reputation
As the evidence was misread
A dire and desperate situation
"I'm innocent" I cry

But the retort is not new
They all say it every day
Regardless if true
I see the bars
I hear the locks
I smell the fear
A miscarriage of justice
An outrage - it's clear
An undeserved life-sentence
No hope of parole
Getting out of here
And, again, reclaiming my life
My one and only goal

Paola Bradley

MY NOVEL

If I could pen a novel
Write a tome to share
Where better to draw inspiration
Than a life well lived
If I dare
Truth is stranger than fiction
I promise not to lie
What better subject
That I know in depth
Than I?
Rags to riches to rags
A wild unfettered ride
An unexpected bookish protagonist
With no earthly place to hide
Glittering career, fall from grace
Disease, abuse, destruction
Catastrophes strike apace
Broken body, broken mind
Adultery and murder
Hidden sins abound
Dark secrets envelop
Ostracism and punishment laid bare
Invisible scars widely found
But woven in the chapters
A message of resilience and hope
That whatever life slings at you
Keep your head...and you will cope

FLYING...

Trapped in reality
The repetitive grind
The daily cycle
Awake, asleep
Awake, asleep
This morning is different
I wake
I stretch
I yawn
Sleep rubbed away
From half open lids
I notice
I puzzle
I feel
Beneath bedclothes
Abnormal additions
Attached to my back
Yet part of me
Warm like my skin
I am not scared
I am curious
I focus
They twitch
I sit up
They unfurl
Iridescent and gossamer
I concentrate
They flutter
I learn

They move faster
They lift me
I hover
I practice
I get stronger
I grow confident
I open the window
And I fly
Finally, free

INFLUENCES

Life is complicated
Tumultuous and taxing
Sometimes introspection lacks bite
And the answers within
Are lacklustre and insufficient
I may own my solutions
And master my own destiny
But I draw inspiration with out
From many sources, not one
The order and creativity of Mother Nature
The wisdom and lived-experience
Of sage parents and grandparents
The ideas and learnings
Of great entrepreneurs
The concepts and teachings
Of philosophers and religious leaders
The wise counsel of trusted friends
A diverse set of influences
Yielding a bounty of knowledge and insight
Not to plagiarise
Not to pilfer
But to borrow from, judiciously
My role to select, sift and sort
Adapt to my needs
Tailor to my context
And apply carefully

So my decisions and actions
Are better informed
And the consequences
Of the choices I make
Are the best they can be

RED CARPET

I sit rolled in a corner
Almost forgotten
Quietly ignored
Crimson velveteen tufts
Densely packed
Underlay visible
Obscuring the majesty
Only ever ceremoniously unfurled
When dignitaries visit
The streets I cover
Usually covered in dust
Dirty and dank
Freshly cleaned
To impress and fool
In the fetid air
The tang of fresh paint
Dingy corners spruced
The homeless ushered away
Children beautifully laundered
Flowers lavishly garlanded
Overflowing bins emptied
So when I am laid out
And smart soles
Tread on my blushing fibres
The illusion is complete
And with my presence
The bare truth hidden

Paola Bradley

Fleetingly...
Till they have gone
And I am rolled away
Then in my absence
The putrid decay
Of real life resumes

FAME

Like a coconut shy
The pedestal an invitation
To find fault
Topple and pillory
Fame the modern obsession
Fifteen minutes in the sun
Now the goal
Not a deserved byproduct
Earned through hard graft
Or god-given talents
Just the limelight
For its own sake
The insane dogged pursuit
Of chasing the dragon
For its addictive temporary high
To find it bites you
And swallows you whole

THE MATCH

I can hear my breath
Blood pounding in my ears
The tune too fast for comfort
My palms unhelpfully moist
Conversely my mouth bone dry
I feel unsteady on my feet
Will my knees give way?
I stifle a cough
All eyes on me
I hate the attention
Is my outfit appropriate?
Too showy, too plain?
Is my hair neat enough?
Do my eyes sparkle?
What do they see
When they look at me?
I feel like an animal
In a gilded cage
...In a market
Will they inspect my teeth?
Count my fingers and toes?
Do they care about my personality?
My desires, my aspirations?
Or do they just see a womb
A cook, a cleaner, a nurse?
The families have conferred
Long ago it was settled
My fate and future decided

I have no say
I have no option
I have no way out
Oppression is duty
Repression a given
Self-conscious, anxious and resigned
My only hope for today...
As I wait nervously
For him to appear
Is that the match made...
...is a good one

CLUTTER

Someone wise once said
"Tidy surroundings, tidy mind"
God knows what that says about me
My shelves piled high
And cupboards straining
With random accumulated debris
That at the time I was convinced
I needed and couldn't do without
Now I was wondering what I was thinking
As I am left to deal with 'owt
Countless nicknacks and trinkets
Glassware, pictures, statues
Mirrors, objects d'art
I regret buying each
Blots on my life
Otherwise sensibly lived
At least, so far
Now I have to sell up
Divest myself of clutter
At the sheer enormity of the task
My horror is more than utter
Each piece holds memories
Some good, some bad, some ugly
But it's time to shed the weight
Of material things amassed glibly
To live a future more streamlined
Unfettered, unencumbered, unburdened
The evidence of a tidy life
Is a demonstrably tidy mind

WRITING

The blank page beckons
Begging for the addition
Of vocabulary and punctuation
Try as I might
To write coherent prose
Somehow the words tumble out
With form and structure
Poetry is more comforting
And flows more easily
Sometimes it rhymes
Sometimes it doesn't
But it always reveals
Far more than I intend
About my mood;
My emotions
My feelings
Which ordinarily go unsaid
And lie far from the surface
Buried beneath
My pen liberates me
Revealing my vulnerabilities
As well as my steely resolve
Hidden, barely concealed
Within my words
You will find
The true me

IF I WERE...

What would I choose to be
If I could be but any
Oh goodness the choices
The options, I have so many
A humble car
A mighty rocket
Or a ship
To sail away quite far
But in truth
It's a helicopter for which I'd opt
With glistening blades aloft
The prized agile feature
Vertical take-off and landing, noch
No more inglorious shunting
Into that tight Brent X parking slot
Determined to beat the queues
I'd zoom to the sales to shop
Shopping frenzy over
Booty safely tucked away
I'd head for my trusty chopper
Perfect for a dedicated shopper
And fly contentedly away

TRADING PLACES?

I'm sitting pondering
Whose life do I covet?
With whom would I trade places?
Who sparkles?
Who has it all?
Who is adored and admired?
Who doesn't struggle?
Whose life is charmed?
Where every day seems easy
And everything falls neatly into place
Great career
Intellectual challenge
Loving family
Supportive friends
Perfect partner
Sterling health
Optimistic prognosis
At a glance
Many seem to fit the bill
Upon closer scrutiny
Cracks are evident
Issues lie behind each facade
Every contender is flawed
And no substitute ideal
Delving into history
Fares no better
All fall disappointingly short

The exercise in imagining
Serving merely to underline
That we should appreciate
The life we are given
And invest energy improving it
Rather than wishing to exchange it
Being proud to wear our shoes
And walk the proverbial mile
Comfortable in our own skin
At peace with our fate
And the person
We see in the mirror

NEW YEAR WISHES

2020 in the rearview mirror
Definitely best in hindsight left
A new year is dawning
Where possibilities abound
The best news of all
A vaccine has been found
My hope for 2021
Is immunity and freedom
For all not just some
An end to social distancing
An end to fragmented family
A reunion of friends
An upturn in the economy
Brexit, Trump and COVID behind us
Heralding a reset to normality
But I also hope we retain
The good things we have gained
Respect for the caring professions
The unconditional help from stangers
A refocus on the necessary
The appreciation of small things
And the majesty of nature
I don't want a wholesale
Return to ways of old
But a modern revised world
A kinder, fairer, wiser planet
A secure future for the next generation
So my rally call for each and every nation

Paola Bradley

Is to step up to the plate
And not leave things too late
To learn from the harsh lessons of 2020
And make 2021
A year of hope, peace and plenty

THAT MOMENT WHEN...

It was an abnormally bright day
Not a cloud in the sky
The sun shining fiercely
An orb way up high
A day of brainstorming
And mental stretching
With leadership at Shell
On the 11th floor
Overlooking the London Eye
The challenge to reshape the business
To better compete and succeed
The kudos for me
I was put in the lead
We took a break
To imbibe coffee, tea
And stretch our legs
In the foyer TV news blaring
Gasps, screams and shouts
A plane entered the building
Like a hot knife in butter
Mobiles started ringing
Panic and stricken horror
The second plane hit
Our brains disbelieved our eyes
The twin towers mortally wounded
Not a tragic accident we concluded
Then the speculation became rife
Was London the next target in sight?

So close to a landmark
We were force to evacuate in fright
No tubes, buses or trains
Every taxi already taken
The city in paralysis
I was forced to walk the long miles home
In ridiculously high heels
Ever checking my phone for updates
I'll never forget
As I walked in the door
Seeing my children
Huddled in front of the screen
At the moment the first tower collapsed
Then the next
How much time had elapsed?
Disbelief and horror
Lives tragically lost
A scar on the city
Perhaps more than that
A day of insight
Into the depravity and courage of man
9/11 who can forget?
I know I never can

COMFORT

When times are rough
And the going gets tough
It's the little things that matter
A luxurious bubble bath
Unctuous body oils
A French manicure
The perfect blow-dry
Fragrant clean sheets
A crisp Rich Tea biscuit
Cheekily smeared with Nutella
Warm soup in a mug
A walk in the park
Fresh breeze on my face
Stopping to marvel at nature
Her bounty, the lush space
A call to friends or family
A kind word or three
A chat about nothing
Just simply being on the line
Is a comfort for me
A gripping thriller
Or comedy to engage
On laptop, phone or TV
Making worries shrink small
The news no longer troubling
Actualities no longer dominating

The silence filled
No room for anxiety
No room for worry
No room for concern
Focus on enjoying today
As tomorrow will look after itself

MISSING?

I don't miss material things
Truth be told
What I miss is my youth
When skin was smooth
Hair was luxuriant
Body was taut
Curves in the right places
Joints didn't creak
Bones didn't ache
Workmen wolf-whistled
Politically incorrect, but pleasant
No mortgage
No pandemic
No Brexit
No Trump
No ugly divorce
Children still in nest
Career booming
Time filled productively
In control of my drama
Not a victim of circumstance
Maybe I am remembering
Through rose tinted specs
And life was as tough then
As it seems to be now
Maybe I was oblivious
Too focused on the minutiae
That I didn't truly see

And what I miss now
Is ephemeral and vapid
A fragile castle of illusions
Perhaps it is better
Not to focus on the lost
But rather to appreciate
The learning and growing gained
To become the person
I am today
And embrace the life
I have now
And am blessed to lead

HUMOUR

Life has a funny way
Of presenting you with opportunities
To step back and laugh
At the absurdities of the moment
Be it the pet or baby
Who inadvertently steals the scene
Acting out in the background
Speaker totally oblivious
To the mayhem unfolding stage left
Or the giggle you have to stifle
When the bigheaded bombastic celebrity
Slips ungainly on the ice
And falls flat on her face
The presenter who always
Mispronounces a name
In a way that sounds rude
Almost shockingly lewd
Or the friend who always
Gets themselves to a mighty pickle
Humorous situations
You could never invent
Life oft stranger than fiction
Slapstick humour abounds
Black comedy beckons
Defying you to keep a straight face
Breaking the mood
Easing the tension
Defusing the situation

Paola Bradley

Mirthful release
What I find funny
May be personal to me
But what has proved universal
Is that laughter is the best medicine

SCHOOL DAY MEMORIES

Poised in the front row
Sitting at the rickety brown desk
Which had seen better days
Knees tucked lightly under
Inkwell full of fresh sharpenings
Hand poised, Parker pen primed
Turquoise ink cartridges
At the front stood the teacher
Auburn ringlets and pashmina
Challenging us to grow our brains
Branching out new synapses
Gorging on knowledge encouraged
Information fizzing
Testing our comprehension
Zoology was my subject
Boring botany banished
The incredible world of animals
Creatures great and small
Fueled my schoolgirl passion
I confess a diabolical pleasure
In detailed dissection
To understand each bone and sinew
Carefully crafted illustrations
Annotated comprehensively and diligently
Little if anything
Directly applies to my life today
What I do take with me
The skill of keen observation

Paola Bradley

Insatiable curiosity
Leaving no stone unturned
And the eternal love
Of learning to learn

GIANTS

We all have unsung heroes
People who have impacted our lives
Made indelible marks
Influenced who we are today
They may not be famous
Or even recognize their contribution
But to us they matter
A wise word shared
Even an off the cuff remark
Can change our trajectory
Make us rethink our path
Make smarter choices
By reframing situations
Through a sharper, clearer lens
The result can be startling
The difference between night and day
To these giants we owe gratitude
For leaving an indelibly positive mark
Illuminating different facets
Clarifying the obscure
Unwittingly, perhaps, they have influenced
And helped shape our destiny
May we follow in their footsteps
And provide this service to others
A virtuous circle
To enrich, to encourage, to enable
There is a giant lurking in us all

Paola Bradley

SATISFACTION

A smug smile
A knowing wink
That feeling that engulfs you
That rosy inner glow
That beams from within
When you have done it
Not necessarily that anyone is looking
No need for tumultuous applause
Nor ostentatious recognition
All that matters
Is that you know
That you tried your best
And put your best foot forward
Pulled off a minor miracle
Made a silk purse
From that dodgy sow's ear
You wove a rich tapestry
From random unmatched threads
You solved the challenging puzzle
Composed the perfect response
Or simply made the perfect cup of tea
Satisfaction, the self-gratification
The proverbial pat on the back
To recognize a job well done
In spite of all obstacles
Relishing in the outcome
And in the knowledge
That today you have truly delivered

LOOKING

I glance furtively
Not sure of what I will see
I squint
Crinkling the corners of my eyes
In the vain hope clarity will emerge
My glasses lenses all blurry
Obscuring my vision not helping
Four eyes no better than two
I try to observe more keenly
Making out each shape
Every nuance in focus
However, looking is but one dimension
Actually seeing is another
Vital difference, not the same
Translating the inputs
Giving meaning
Fostering understanding
But how often do we look
But not actually see?
We jump to conclusions
Filling in the blanks
Missing obvious cues and clues
We see what we expect to see
Not what is really there
Our eyes may be faithful soldiers
But our brain hijacks messages
From the optical battlefield

Tricking us
Fooling us
Deceiving us
It helps to be vigilant
To question what we surmise
And challenge what is reported
By our too oft trusted eyes

WISHES

As I sit here pondering
Thinking about my life
The blessings and the woes
I recognize the hand I've been dealt
Neither perfect nor calamitous
A mixture of rough and tumble
What could I want for
What do I need
An end to acrimony
An end to strife
For me personally
An end to being a wife
Bigger than that
Rude health a necessity
No more pain nor suffering
No pandemic ravaging
Instead I wish for a brighter future
One of diplomacy and tact
Where care for the planet and fellow man
Becomes not ideology but fact
A world where we can live together peacefully
Where brother upholds brother
And we strive for harmony wherever we can
No more wars
No more destruction
Respect for Mother Earth
An ethos of love, respect, shared mirth
As I sit here pondering still

I awaken to the realization
That wishing on a star is futile
Hoping above hope absurd
The power to change the future
Lies firmly in my hands
The only way my wishes can come true
Is if I am the author of my destiny
I drive and control the narrative
It is I who holds the final word
To live a today I can endure
And a tomorrow I can be proud of

ACHIEVEMENT

Some people crave awards
Certificates and medals
To outwardly portray
The battles and strife
That they have fought and overcome
Throughout their life
Some people seek labels
Like job titles
And smart salutations
Like OBE, Sir or Dame
To embellish themselves
Not merely a name
Primped, plumped and proud
For all to behold
To marvel, to admire
Subliminally we are taunted
To applaud and laud
Achievements blatantly flaunted
But isn't it true
That the greatest reward comes from inside
Not out
The warm glow of knowing
You have tried your hardest
You have conquered your fears
You have continued to succeed
Despite advancing years
No need for accolades
No need for the fancy label
You have already proved yourself
Definitely more than able

LIGHT

The future may seem uncertain
The path ahead obscure
We are challenged daily
With every shifting rules
And somber foreboding news
The potential always looming
To feel sad and cheated fools
In spite of the darkness
And the brooding horizon
Small things serve to illuminate
To light the path ahead
Making living more bearable
Fostering hope for tomorrow instead
A tender smile
A baby's gurgle
A handwritten letter
A stranger's kindness
Dewdrops on petals
Shimmering and glistening
A double rainbow piercing the grey
All unexpected tiny pleasures
To brighten a dismal day
A glass half empty
Turned to be half full
Perhaps the greatest lesson
Is fate may write the script

But we own the voice
And subtle inflection
To shape the hand we are dealt
It is we who are the masters
To dictate a life well spent

COPING STRATEGIES

Would't it be lovely if life were a smooth ride
Only an upward trajectory
No bumps on the path
Only rainbows and silver linings
No drudgery nor disappointment
No mishaps nor melancholy
No brickbats, just bouquets
Sadly, the landscape is more haphazard
A combination of swings and roundabouts
Pepper our daily horizon
To cope with this treacherous terrain
A metaphoric backpack is needed
Stuffed with band aids for grazed knees
But also wounded pride
A tin of canned laughter
To prise open and release mirth
When sorely needed
Or prick the lid
And pop open a reassuring smile
To ease the tension
And prompt us to relax
A virtual photo album
Buried deep
Capturing old memories
Images of brighter days
To remind us of better times
But also keep us hopeful

These can indeed return
A golden bow and arrow
Nestled safely within
To ensure we keep aiming for the stars
A forcefield to insulate
And protect us from the worst
A prism to refocus and deflect
And colour each situation more kindly
Tucked away in the front pocket
An instant sachet of courage
Mixed liberally with hope
And a pair of spring soled sneakers
To equip us to survive today
And bounce back to thrive tomorrow

Paola Bradley

TREASURED PHOTO

Hear no evil
See no evil
Say no evil
The elegant trio
Mutual love unwritten
Understood by the pose
Tenderly interlocked arms
Natural and unstilted
Not artifice for the photo
Three peas in a pod
Different but alike
Ripened and matured
No longer babes
But assured adults
All grown and confident
My greatest success
My most precious assets
They far outweigh any other
Knowing eyes belie wisdom
Far greater than their years
The girls resplendent
Fitted bejeweled gowns
The boy, no man
Perfectly penguin suited
Three perfect specimens
External beauty
Radiating from goodness within
Smiles and happiness palpable

Celebration of a wedding
A union, heralding family expansion
The catalyst for the next generation
To branch out and grow
A time of shared joy
Reverie and salutation
Far greater than the sum
Of its parts
Always in a frame nearby
Watching over me
But the image yet
Ever etched in my mind

Paola Bradley

MY FAVOURITE MEAL

Write an ode to a sausage
Or celebrate haggis in elaborate prose
Laud a poached egg oozing temptingly
Or kippers wafting pungently
Why these come to mind
God only knows!
Humble cheese toastie
Tarted up with onion jam
Goats cheese and beetroot salad
Garnished with basil and marjoram
And a squirt of balsamic glaze
A generous one
If I can
101 ways with chicken
Griddled, curried and stir-fried
A crisp assortment of vegetables
Arranged neatly on the side
A tangle of spaghetti
Smothered in rich Bolognese
If I plan carefully
Enough to last 3 days
Truth be told
Starter and main course
I would happily forgo
Skip straight to dessert
But my waistline would grow
Calorie-laden treats
Consumed not for nutritional value

But for mouthfeel
And a sharp sugar high
Eton mess, sticky toffee pudding
I wish I could force myself
To love all things less sweet
Because after all
We are what we eat

Paola Bradley

An Extra Hour

I find my days interminable
When I wake
And I shake the sleep from my eyes
I sigh
Another day stretching ahead
I wonder
How will I fill it?
How can I make the best of my time
And what will I have to show for it
When my head hits that pillow again
I struggle to fill my hours as it is
Drawing, painting, writing
Reading, cooking, cleaning
Zooms thankfully punctuate and give purpose
But I have the attention span of a gnat
And a miniscule boredom threshold
Every day is Groundhog Day
Doing the same routine
Just different clothes
Freshly applied makeup and coiffed hair
An extra hour for many would be a blessing
For me simply a curse
Sixty long more minutes to fill
Three thousand six hundred aching seconds
I feel it every year
When the clock turns back
And we are given the gift of time
I envy those who use it productively

Learn an instrument or a new language
Make space to engage with friends
Or give back to the community
This exercise has made me stop and think
And analyse what I fritter time on
Time to break the cycle
And realise time is precious
But also finite and never repeated
Time to make every hour count

PERCEPTION AND PUDDLES

Beauty is in the eye of the beholder
Clothes maketh the man
Never judge a book by its cover
All that glitters is not gold
All these proverbs challenge us
The gauntlet is our perception
We use our senses
Sound
Sight
Smell
Taste
Touch
To make sense of the world around us
To simplify the chaos
To tame the noise
We shortcut the complex
To codify and comprehend
But can we really trust ourselves?
There isn't one truth
There are often many
Depending on your vantage point
Perception and reality not equal bedfellows
Philosophers wrestle with these concepts
Illusion, reality, fact and artifice
There are no hard lines
Rather murky puddles between them
Opinion, culture and society act as distorting lenses
Through which we view and appraise

Two witnesses – one event
Two valid explanations
If you step in each's shoes
Not a matter of right or wrong
Purely a matter of perception
Too often we jump to conclusions
Or apply our own filter to facts
Do we ever ponder the alternative view?
We jump on differences of opinion
Without considering why
Life is rarely black or white
Much is open to interpretation
Diversity and inclusion
Not merely a trendy label
But a call for us to question
Why views are polarized
Why there is dissent
Why there is unrest
It all starts with us
It doesn't lie with others
As you sow, so shall you reap
Actions speak louder than words

Paola Bradley

SPRING IS ON THE WAY

The days get slowly longer
Less need to switch on the light
The days are getting warmer
Less need for layers
And wrapping up tight
The cherry blossom is appearing
Festooning the avenues and mews
Dormant buds blooming
Garlands of crocuses encircling
Trees as they start to bud
Carpets of saluting daffodils
To hail the new season
Winter long behind us
Lazy summer yet to be courted
Frisky animals gambol
Libido ignited and awakened
Mother's Day and Easter
The clock set forwards
New shoots, new beginnings
A heralding of possibilities
The annual cycle rests
As nature refreshes, so can we
With the slate wiped clean
We too can reinvent ourselves
And tackle life
With renewed vim and vigor
Mother Nature teaching us

That fresh starts are possible
Time to embrace the valuable lessons
Then for each and every one of us
Spring will truly have sprung

Paola Bradley

REALITIES

Wistful childhood innocence
The tender memories
Of halcyon days
Illuminated softly
The past glorified
Enhanced in technicolour
Vaseline lens smeared
Airbrushed and edited
Yesterday's sweet remembrance
In contrast the present
Challenging and sharp
Complexity, raw emotions
Flaws and issues tangible
Grappling with obstacles
Battling each step
To survive every today
And realise a better tomorrow
Yesterday long gone

HER MARK

A crimson defined lip
Expertly manicured fingers
A pristine crisp collar
Well maintained leather pumps
A puff of dandy fur
Scattered sequins sparkle
A polished bob cut jauntily
The baroque pearl choker
An emerald cut ring
Tweed jacket fitting snugly
Trimmed with sumptuous velvet
The scent of heaven
No curse words
No crude jokes
More sarcasm and irony
Enriched with elegant adjectives
In one language...or three
Smart phrases to engage
Witticisms tumble
Classy repartee abounds
With a knowing wink and twinkle
She captures your heart
She captures your soul
A modern enigma
A perennial addition to our midst
A nod to a time gone by
When grace and beauty ruled

Now long gone
But still here she stands
A paragon
A role model
Her wrinkles insignificant
Softened by fine powder
Knowing dark eyes
Betray intellect and wisdom
A woman of valour
A woman of worth
Grandma, I love you

SUFFERING

Words don't do it justice
Gnawing, burning, gnarling
Angry crimson, vermillion red
Flames consume
Deep within
Tissues straining
Sinews afire
Muscles clenched
Pain uncontrollable
Tearing and sparring
Jarring discomfort
Tearful agony
Overwhelming angst
Each movement exquisite
Carefree activity thwarted
Every move a deliberation
A careful calculation
Is it worth the suffering?
Do I really need it?
Plan surrendered
To unexpected immobility
Time stretching forward
Uncertain recovery horizon
Trust ceded to the body
To heal and repair
Patience never a virtue
Makes today ever more raw
And tomorrow uncertain

Paola Bradley

MEDICAL MIRACLE – OUCHBEGONE

A test tube of wishes
Starlight suspended
Gossamer wisps of enigma
Powdered hope from a jar
Kisses crumbled in for good measure
No doctor needed
No chemical concoctions
Just mix liberally with motherly love
Apply with tender care
Add comforting words
In a tone to caress
Rashes vanish
Sores disappear
Pain soothed
Malady obliterated
Fever abated
Ouch subsides
Cheeks reflush a healthy pink
Tears all dried
Smiles reinstalled
Ready to play again

AUTUMN

Conkers burnished bright
Rust, orange, golden leaves
Trees laden in technicolour glory
With added texture and crispness
Term-time resumed
New shoes shining
Blazers too big
Bought to grow into
New year heralded in
Apple and honey
Thoughts of sins past
Asking forgiveness
The celebration of life
Summer fading in a haze
Nights drawing in
An extra jumper
Warm thermal vests
Socks happily refound
Duvet pulled over
Dawn chorus later
The view from the window changes
The full spectrum foliage
Squirrels colour-matched
Crops begging harvest
Mother earth bountiful
Providing sustenance and choice
Nature truly triumphs

Paola Bradley

LOCKDOWN HOLY DAYS

New year, new beginnings
The reset button
Heralded by the shofar
Normally in a packed shul
This year from afar
Apple dipped in honey
Raisin studded loaves
Pomegranate seeds of hope
Custom to feast together
Challenged by new rules
Definition of community strained
This year belonging reconsidered
No rabbi dressed in white
No need for new outfits
To mark the celebration
In our sweatpants seek forgiveness
Our sins laid bare
Asking for absolution
Seeking repentance
Spirituality now internal
Within rather than without
We focus alone
On the consequences of our actions
And hope to receive
The holy gift of light

New Year, Pandemic-style

Fading days of summer
A golden illuminated scene
Heralding this new year
Not the same as every other
New traditions needed
A different interpretation
To celebrate and observe
A select group of relatives
Not exceeding six
Share the feasting table
No extended family
No hugs nor kisses
Apple still weds honey
Sticky honey cake
Shofar in the park, not Shul
Zoom a very useful tool
This year we celebrate creatively
Merely the spirit of the holyday preserved
The essence and intention
Of Rosh Hashanah distilled
Yesteryear's tradition reimagined
Made relevant for our today

UNEXPECTED

The doorbell rings
My mind races wildly
My eyes turn to the skies
My heart beats a little faster
Sweat dampens my brow
An unexpected pleasure
A surprise event
An unusual occurrence
I am barely prepared
My hair a little messy
My outfit crumpled
My cupboards relatively bare
How will I receive you?
Welcome arms
A smile
Carefully curated chat
Dare I say gossip
Plumped up cushions
Your space reserved
A perfect cup of tea
Scattered chocolate digestives
I may not have expected you
But you are always a welcome pleasure

MEDIA INSPIRATION

Life can appear stranger than fiction
But from the arts we can definitely learn
Scenarios and sonnets by Shakespeare
Events dreamed up by Dickens and Chaucer
Classic poems like the Iliad and Odessey
All present parallels or parables
From which to draw today
No current situation completely new
Even frothy rom-coms
Disney enchanted tales
Or the daily soaps on which we binge
Subliminally teach us new lessons
Which can be applied here and now
We think we are unique
But there is nothing new under the sun
Perhaps the most comprehensive
A collection of valuable lessons
In the humble bedside bible
Stories galore, set in days of yore
Heroes and villains
Battles and strife
Temptation, sin, salvation
Human relations laid bare
Morality and mortality explored
The distance between then
And now shortened
A text to study and savour
Not just stories
To be told at cheder

Paola Bradley

THE TELEPHONE

The black bakelite unit
The clunky plastic dial
Numbers and letters
The curly coiled lead
The enamel scarlet phone box
Coins jingling at the ready
Dial "O" for operator
Prepare to connect
Brace yourself for reverse charges
They may or may not accept
Standing in a smelly corner
Waiting for the answer
Who could have predicted
Who could have guessed
Here in the 2020s
These icons would be replaced
By a slim black wafer
More than a diary
More than an address book
More than a calculator
More than an encyclopaedia
More intelligence in your pocket
Than the president had in 1994
Every tune reachable
A theme for every occasion
Gratuitous games galore
Even payments in a click

Our definition of telephone has shifted
No longer merely a communication tool
For reaching family and friends
Now a miniaturized computer
Essential to our lives
Fitting snugly in our lives
A portal to the possible
But increased connectedness is an illusion
We are ever more dependable
Memory becomes expendable
The excuse for proximity removed
Messages replace the need for touch
We have never been more alone

NEVER...

Never let a stumble
Be the end of a journey
Metaphoric backpack loaded
Resources securely tucked within
Onwards and upwards
Striving for a brighter future
Every step calculated
For better or for worse
Every word and breath measured
Direction never in reverse
Inevitable are the stumbles
The grazes on the way
Life's perennial hurdles
Buffeting our trajectory
Fortitude is overcoming
Dusting ourselves off regardless
Taking the good from the bad
Continuing our journey
A little older
A little wiser
Wounded but not thwarted
Rather stronger for the battle
The ultimate goal
Unshakably within grasp
The scars of yesterday
Valuable badges of honour
Learnings visible for all to see
Each today another victory scored
The foundation to a better tomorrow

HANGING ON THE LINE

I've been through the damned menu
Listening to the stupid options
Pressing 1,2 or three
I've been patient till now
But my anger is boiling
I'm enraged – can't you see
I'm tapping my leg furiously
Drawing increasingly rabid scribbles
Number 15 in the queue
Really, a flood of callers
At the exact same time as me?
I've picked the rush hour for audio-traffic
It seems, unfortunately
I'm at the end of my tether
No keeping me temper in check
I know, my bad
I know when you answer
You'll be following a script
Like an automaton on autopilot
Caring for me not a jot
Till then the interminable muzac
As you keep me on hold
I wish I didn't need to speak to you
If the truth be told
But here I am hanging
Dangling annoyingly on the line
Waiting like an idiot
Till the line you choose to answer
Is finally mine

Paola Bradley

Desert Island Dreaming

If I were stranded
On a remote deserted isle
I'd opt to take six things with me
Chosen purely to make me smile
First, I'd take a butler
To bow and serve and press
Then to impress the natives
I'd take my bestest dress
A fine bone china tea-set
Dainty cups of tea to quaff
And a comfy hammock
To balance between palms
A kind of bed, aloft
Fifth a Jo Malone candle
For a gently fragrant waft
Last a well-stocked album
Photos of friends and family I miss
Company and memories
To forget would be remiss
In this flight of fancy
My choices totally impractical
Better a swiss army knife, phone
Mosquito net, first aid kit and lighter
Than these fripperies and nonsense
Only designed to make life brighter
But truth be told, I'm a dreamer
And thoughts of survival distant
What springs to mind right now
Reveals my true nature
In an instant

CLUTTER

My heart sinks
As I look round the room
I wonder what I was thinking
I have accumulated so much
At the time each piece was researched
A bargain as I mentally calculated potential profit
But rather than selling I moved to the next
The palpable excitement as the postman came
Laden with enticing brown parcels
But as I look today at this treasure
I realise the folly of my ways
No one is interested in this detritus
The naïve Inuit carvings
Intricate French perfume bottles
Or towers of dainty tea-sets
Paintings, sculptures, vases, boxes
Was there anything I didn't collect
I remember it made me happy
But it also caused huge arguments
"We are neither a museum nor a bank"
Ghosts of accusations haunt me
Now I am surrounded by my folly
Unneeded, unloved artefacts
Holding me back from moving forward
Building resentment and regret
Finding a home for them
Better still converting then to much needed cash

Increasingly unlikely in this climate
Everyone is downsizing, sorting and decluttering
Perhaps I need to take a brave step
And black bag this noise
To be able to step into my future
Somewhat lighter and finally unburdened

GIVING SUPPORT

Uplifting purpose giving me hope
When I thought all was lost
Sustenance was at hand
Defying gravity
Discouraging laxity
Beyond charity
A firm foundation
A helping hand
Structuring chaos
An engineering marvel
Supporting the unsupportable
Hoisting the droopy
Cupping the fallen
Providing comfort and solace
Ensuring all present and correct
And pointing in the right direction
Worthy of an Oscar
For best supporting actor
Creating a wonderous edifice
Perfect to behold
My bra is invaluable to me
If the truth be told

DREAM CRUISE

A large ocean liner
Staff dressed in crisp white
A floating luxury hotel
With a fancy cabin for the night
Choppy seas make me queasy
Life aboard all too easy
One luxury banquet to another
Captains table lavish
Breakfast lunch and dinner
The pomp and circumstance
Feeling like a lottery winner
A delectation of ports to visit
Edited highlights of the Med
Rome, Haifa, Naples and Athens
Tourist honeypots all
If the truth be said
Crumbling ancient ruins
Picture postcard perfect landmarks
Art galleries and museums galore
Bustling thriving markets
What's not to adore
Each day a different country
A different language
A different flavor
Dream destinations ticked
A bucket list bonanza
A toe barely dipped

Eight lands in eight days
Exactly as the itinerary says
Staged managed to perfection
But pay close attention
How truly authentic
Has the experience really been
And what is it actually
That we haven't yet seen

Paola Bradley

MINUS MOBILE

What would I do without my mobile
That portable thin black wafer
Which now rules my life
No calendar
No news streaming
No games to distract
No Dr Google
Where would I find
The answers to random questions
That plague me day and night
And find all the numbers
For my nearest and dearest
My memory has become lazy
Relying on stored contacts
Rather than filed in my brain
Instant gratification, akin to Pavlov's mutt
Keep me reaching for that pocket near my butt
I have become used to instant information
My impatience sated time and time again
With it I feel connected
Photos and videos of extended family
A close proxy to being there
Now the pandemic and busy life
Precludes physical proximity
When it occasionally crashes
Probably from exhaustion
From extreme overuse
My heart sinks

Till the reset succeeds
And that white apple appears
On a seemingly dead screen
I admit my dependence
I am hooked – that's my vice
Better than booze, fags or drugs
But an addiction all the same
In comparison the transgression
Seems somewhat tame
My phone has become indispensable
A friend, a toolkit, a crutch
A single hour without it
Has become sixty minutes too much

Paola Bradley

TEA TIME

I wonder how it started
The daily ritual
Kettle filled with fresh water
Best big mug at the ready
Teabag steeped not stewed
Till the exact Dulux shade
Tangy tannins well-brewed
Should the dash of milk
Be before or after
Which is polite
Does it really matter
If you get the colour exactly right
It's hard to give up sugar
That one spoon does it for me
Sweetener may be kinder on the waistline
But mars the taste you see
Piping hot burns my mouth
So, I let it cool a little first
Like little bear on Goldilocks
Not too cool, not too hot
Leave it too long
And isn't the same
Sorry, I just forgot
I love my daily cuppa
To drink it alone, a shame
Better shared with friends
Better accompanied by a biscuit
Dunked till moist not soggy
Funny how comforting it can be
To make and drink the perfect cup of tea

WHEN LOCKDOWN IS OVER

And life begins to tick back
The person I want to sit next to
And listen to intently
Is my grandfather
Who would have been 110 this week
An incorrigible bigamist
An astonishing intellect
Professor, architect
Accordion playing tap dancer
Eyes sparkling blue
Just like Paul Newman
Brain the size of a planet
No fun too outrageous
No joke too blue
Stories tumbled from his lips
Like sticks in a waterfall
His leathered face
Distinguished not aged
His roman nose statuesque
What wisdom
What humour
What passion for life
He loved women, all women
My brothers dismissed in the corner
I was his focus
The clothes he designed for me
The conversations we shared
The consulate dinner party and house guest

Sparkling repartee
Raconteur extraordinaire
Open-mind listener
Who better to share tomorrow with
Than a man who I adored
And who loved me unconditionally

SOMETIMES IT IS THE SMALLEST DETAIL...

The inconspicuous that gives it away
The wrinkle at the corner of your eye
The slight curl on your lip
The altered tone in your voice
You try to hold it in
Keep the secret safe within
But your body betrays you
Leaking signs
That contradict your conversation
Some may overlook
Others adept at perception
Will notice each incongruence
And turn it into an opportunity
To better match their offering
Consciously or unconsciously
Morphing their responses
To better suit your mood
And receptivity
With consumate ease
The dance of persuasion
A naked truth
Your cues beyond words
Leading your conclusion
Unknowingly
Unwittingly
The silent clues you broadcast
Responsible for your fate

I HAD TO DO IT

It was winking at me
I couldn't ignore it
The temptation too great
Desire burning uncontrollably
I tried to forget it
But it gnawed my consciousness
Tugging at the sleeve of my attention
Distraction failing dismally
Pretending it wasn't there was doomed
I had promised myself to leave it
My willpower now a withered husk
Compelled to succumb
Any resistance was futile
Logic dwarfed by emotion
The devil whispering in my left ear
Far outsmarted the angel on my right
I had to do it...
...I had to eat the last Rolo

THE BREAK

Ironic that the break
Begat her break
Mousy brown
In the chorus line
Third row from the back
Throwing envious glances
At the leading lady
All glory and accolades
Pirouettes and solos
Applause unbounded
Why not me?
That fateful night
A careless stumble
Unsafe props
An unfortunate angle
Forcing a fracture
And exit stage left
An empty spotlight
Top billing wanting
The opportunity to step up
To transform and sparkle
And take centre stage
Though under the greasepaint
Her guilt barely disguised
Not pat superstition
But sincerely said
The meteoric rise triggered
By her prophetic wish
To break a leg

BEDTIME

The daylight fades
Limbs heavy and weary
Energy spent
Bones, muscles and sinews
Achingly needing rest
Bathtime ritual sacrosanct
Unguents and potions
Limbs and face smothered
Skin clean and fragrant
Mattress inviting
Slumber beckons
Fertile dreams await
Head on silk pillow
All plumped and warm
Eyelids heavy
Daily drudgery forgotten
Rhythmic calmed breathing
Slowing of mind
Thoughts pass through
Rather than linger
Like clouds blown by a breeze
Sounds fade in the distance
Today's cares wash away
I am ready to embrace sleep
For tomorrow is another day

CHRISTMAS

Fairy lights twinkling
Log fire roaring
Striped stockings hanging
Tree bedecked, all proud
Presents wrapped neatly
Carols sung sweetly
Table heaving with festive fare
A feast of delicacies to share
And gorge on if we dare
Bought for three families
But now whittled to only us
We try not to be affected
Try not to make a fuss
Nose pressed to window expectantly
Waiting impatiently
Outside snowflakes dance and sparkle
Whipped up like a dervish furiously
Fuelled by the wild and wanton wind
Settling finally on the crisp snowy frosting
That frames the Yuletide scene
A snowman guards the garden
Wizened carrot nose and scarlet scarf
Robin perched precariously atop
The seasonal sentinel for Santa
Disguised today as the Amazon man
Laden with the late brown parcels
He wrestles from his white van
The virus temporarily forgotten

A day of joy and celebration
The queen's carefully scripted speech
Pulling together the nation
Xmas plans may have been shaken
But sentiments unashamedly retained
Joy, peace, family and appreciation
Focused not on what we've lost this year
But on what we've sincerely gained

THE FUTURE

Who knows what lurks around the corner
What twists and turns await
The one thing of which we can be certain
Is our very uncertain fate
Don't be complacent
And expect the inclement
You will be blown off course
You will be tempted astray
You will encounter hurdles
Inevitable along the way
The measure of a man
Or indeed a woman
Not achievement per se
But resilience demonstrated
And ability to adapt
To overcome and thrive
Rather than being frustrated
Grasping the nettle
Keep persisting
Ignoring obstacles
Evolving and adapting
Striving and conquering
Riding the waves
Not succumbing
Mastery of the future
Favours the brave

THE SALES

Who can resist a bargain
A bin end
A seemingly huge markdown
How clever they are
To tempt us
With things we don't really need
That red sticker
The blue cross
The word sale
Irresistible magnets
Luring us in
Beckoning brazenly
Blinding us to abandon judgement
Forcing our wallets open
Bending our credit cards beyond limits
For that thing in the wrong colour
Not exactly the right fit
That gadget we have no use for
The toy that will stay in its box
Budget and planning all forgotten
As we fight our way to the tills
And queue endlessly
Basket and trolleys
Brimming with nonsense
Convinced all is vital
And excellent value
All year we scrimp and save
And apply thoughtful judgment

Spending calculated and measured
Black Friday changes all that
Mesmerising,enticing and bewitching
Shopping becomes an annual sport
One we can not resist to partake
The only rules are spending and splurging
Gorging on the unnecessary
With retailers the only winners
When will we learn?

SHE

I look in her eyes
And what do I see
But a version of myself
And you
Looking back at me
Not a carbon copy
But familiar features
My almond eyes
Your upturned nose
Familial full cheeks
Skin tone a shade between
Hands like mine
Toes like yours
Beyond structure
Does DNA explain
Shared mannerisms and tastes
The looks she throws
Her favourite foods
Her pet hates
Sometimes typically maternal
Sometimes wholly paternal
Nature and nurture combined
Encapsulated in her we see
Reflections and echoes
An intoxicating blend of you and me

PROGRESS

The world turns
Button on fast forward
Staying still requires momentum
Obsolescence a recurring reality
Operating in today's paradigm
Is is insufficient armour
To fend tomorrow's challenge
Each day we push a little further
Ten more metaphorical steps
Exercising parts otherwise dormant
Exploring new possibilities
Challenging ourselves
Not only to keep up
But to push forwards
And make progress
So when we lie on our pillows at night
We can relax with self-satisfaction
Knowing that we did our best
To keep up and forge forward
Never again to be left behind

Paola Bradley

STAYCATION

Borders shut, seclusion enforced
The lure of a sojourn abroad quashed
No palm fringed beaches
No foreign markets to explore
Nor historic sites to visit
Instead holidays take a different shape
Forced to define leisure closer to home
The break opportunity on our doorstep
Long overlooked treasures are noticed
Reasons why foreign tourists flock revealed
At our fingertips glorious lush countryside
Stately homes, museums, galleries
Historic significance in every corner
Local restaurants in every flavour
Bed and board for every pocket
Amusement parks galore
The benefit of a common language
The only disappointment inclement weather
Adds dimension to dialogue
A national obsession we all partake in
No long flight back
No jet lag to contend with
This year we were force to realise
There is no place like home

GROWING OLDER

Hairline receding slightly
Waistline a little thicker
Gravity winning the battle
A few centimetres conceded
Even when walking proud
Hearing less acute
Necessitating the TV turned up loud
Eyes needing brighter light
Small print now a challenge
A world through four lenses
No longer two, especially at night
Joints a little rustier
Movement less fluid
Skin a little saggier
"Less firm" more polite
Settling in grooves and furrows
No longer snapping back
White and random hair sprouting
On head, from nose, in ears and on chin
The body the battleground scars of advancing years
A war we will never win
The mind and mood another matter
Age the superhero variable
Calmer, more sanguine
Experience and wisdom to the fore
A knowing wink and smile
Having done it, got the t shirt before
Random knowledge twinned with insight

TV quizzes a breeze
Navigating life's necessary turbulence
With greater confidence and ease
Youth is not to envy
Advancing years we should embrace
The folly of the young
Firmly in the rear-view mirror
We stand as time flies past us
Knowing a more contented future awaits

THE GOOD OLD DAYS

It's all too easy
To reminisce and languish in memories
Our mind tricks us
Rose coloured filter
Applied to events past
Negatives replaced with positives
Significant details omitted
Facts artfully edited
Festooning flourishes added
The canvas reworked
The narrative nudged
Remembrance airbrushed
Our role as protagonist enhanced
So yesteryear reappears with fondness
Illuminated with a soft romantic glow
Enhancing all things past
Thus we yearn for a return
To an illusion of time long gone
If only we could focus
And expend the same mental energy
Creating a positive present
And a future filled with promise
Stop clinging to the ephemeral "good old days"
Make your today count every day
And invest energy wisely in your tomorrow

Paola Bradley

RISE AND SHINE

Burrowed beneath billowing bedding
Eyes strain to lift leaden lids
Sleepy slumber
Summarily shaken off
Dreams disengaged
Reality recognised
A glance at the clock
To check it is really morning
And the day can begin
A stretch and a yawn
The body unfurled
Ready to rinse and repeat
The cycle of daily rituals
And chores
With vim and vigour
Oh, how we strive
To embrace and conquer
Each today with fresh eyes
With keen hope
And good intent
Till spent,
Time and energy melts away
And sleep again
Heralds another tomorrow
And a farewell to this day

THE LAST CORNETTO

The sound unmistakable
The tinkling nursery tune
Repeating endlessly
Piercing yet pleasing
Colouring the daily hubbub and drudgery
Catnip to children and adults alike
Swarms congregating
Untidy raggedy queues
Impatiently yet politely waiting their turn
Marvelling at the tempting selection
Favourite sugar-laden target in their sights
Notes and coins at the ready
Waistbands loosened in anticipation
Vivid rainbow coloured lollies
Copious whipped and swirled dairy concoctions
Straddling wafer cones defying gravity
Festooned with sprinkles
And the extravagant flourish of a flake
Commercial brands also available
For those less adventurous
Comfort eating the familiar
A "safer" more conservative option
Wedded to my sensible choice
Eagerly awaiting my indulgent treat
My heart sinks
My disappointment palpable
As through the van's serving window
The little boy in front of me
Is handed the last blooming Cornetto

Paola Bradley

MY FIRST LOVE

You captured my heart
Right from the first instant
Strong broad shoulders
Toned firm body
Lean and so tall
To me you seemed a giant
In stature and standing
But it was the details that got me
The small pulsing vein on your temple
Your mischievous knowing eyes
Paved with tiny crinkles as you smiled
They stirred and warmed my soul
Your huge leathered hands
Capable of so much
But mine to hold
Your deep gentle voice
Every utterance precious
You made me believe I was special
You made me believe I was beautiful
You made me believe I was invincible
You protected me
You adored me
You shaped me
I loved you
I worshipped you
I trusted you
I believed you
Now you are gone

You are far from forgotten
I see your legacy in the mirror
I hear myself saying your words
Doing things you would
The apple falls never far from the tree
My first love, my daddy

Lightning Source UK Ltd.
Milton Keynes UK
UKHW010713160223
417123UK00005B/355